They Might Be Toxic

Maria Colomy

DEDICATION

This book is dedicated to all the women and men who made it out, and to all the women and men who will.

CONTENTS

ACKNOWLEDGMENTS

To my friend Pilar, who reached out one day for a discussion, and ended up lighting a fire.

To all the abusive, demeaning, unhealed souls who helped me write this book. Without you, I would never know my own tenacity, my own strength, or my own will.

And of course, I'd like to thank me, for my own hard work, for loving myself enough to get out, and stay out. May the bridges we burn light our way.

Introduction

"Toxic" – the blanket label that has become ever-so-popular for any and all things that we find unpleasant. Right?

Well not here. Beyond the sarcasm and hyperbole, in this text I'll be addressing one very specific thing, truly toxic, harmful behavior that you may be pacifying because you THINK you're being polite, keeping the peace, or whatever other co-dependent excuse you've chosen.

This is not a how-to manual. I am not a therapist. This is a guide for those who can't seem to spot the traits until it's too late – because I am one of you – and even though I jokingly say I'm a Narc Ninja, the reality is that I'm not. If I were I wouldn't need to write this book.

- I'm slightly more aware.
- I react slightly faster than I used to.
- I recognize the behavior much faster than I used to.
- I am still in recovery.
- Detoxing, if you will.

The tough thing about learning is that once you do it, you want to teach everyone what you know. We suddenly think that because we've walked the path, we're now an expert. Others may think that too.

The even more difficult thing is that unsolicited advice is not only unwelcome, but also rarely received, heard, or considered.

But let's say that you love your best friend, sibling, co-worker, and there's just no way to tell them what you're seeing. All the buzzwords – narcissism, codependency do not sound like what they really are.

Someone who doesn't know the traits of narcissism, or the clinical diagnosis narcissistic personality disorder or NPD may assume we're talking about simple vanity. Even as I type this – Microsoft Word is defining it as "self-love and vanity" – only slightly laughable. The term co-dependency sounds like nothing more than a very dependent relationship – and while that can be one aspect of codependency, it is truly a multi-faceted, and very scripted set of behaviors that I will leave to other experts on the subject.

There are countless YouTube series, books, and podcast if you care to get into the dirty details, which, as you unfold your own story may be a natural part of your own learning process like it has been for the countless hundreds of thousands before you, before me.

Dr. Ramani Durvasula, whose work I love, says that codependency and narcissism are the second-hand smoke of mental health issues. Being around them is going to affect your health eventually. To see her videos look up "Dr. Ramani" on YouTube. She has a ton of great free content, plus paid courses and a podcast, and has been a great source of learning for me in my own series of toxic relationships.

I am grateful to the many content creators on YouTube and SoundCloud who've helped me to learn – the other two who are notable for me are Richard Grannon and Lisa A. Romano.

Just know that the information you need as you go through this discovery will show up as you need it. You will find your favorite presenters on the subject.

There is no one way to heal – there are infinite ways to heal.

Let's get to why you're here – to answer your own questions. Are they toxic? Is this situation toxic? This job, this family, *this whatever* – is it a healthy relationship or is it robbing me of my peace? The first answer is – trust your gut, trust yourself.

They might be toxic if:

1. You were deeply, deeply charmed, but once you got in it felt like a bait & switch.
2. You're not allowed to have friends, your own free time, your own money.
3. You're not allowed privacy, alone time, and you're simply not trusted.
4. You are discouraged or sabotaged from self-improvement plans and efforts.
5. The relationship is based on unsolicited advice or having aspects of your life managed by someone else.
6. Apologies come in the form of promises, material goods or money, and not in the form of changed behavior, real discussions, or real change.
7. There is no room for your opinion or any outside viewpoints in discussions.
8. You are baited with progressively more intrusive questions until you're being bullied for something you've shared.
9. You feel unsafe sharing good news, future plans, new ideas, or even bad news.
10. You are expected to know what the person wants without ever being told, and then punished for not reading their mind.
11. You are expected to be okay with any form of abusive behavior toward yourself or others.

THEY MIGHT BE TOXIC

Chapter 1

Charmed To Meet You

Chapter 1: Charmed To Meet You

Sometimes we are born with the toxic people in our lives. For most of us that's where it starts; one or both of our parents and one or more of our siblings, and oftentimes grandparents. Growing up it might be a neighborhood bully, a teacher, a coach.

We will learn by the age of 10 what to expect from relationships. These formative years affect our future lives. You either have safety or you don't, and then, you either expect safety – or you don't.

The hard part of this dynamic is that often as kids we fantasize about a rescue, our prince charming who will come along, and everything will be right in the world. Our fantasy job, our fantasy life tends to put others as the hero in the story.

This charming hero will have all the answers. Your future will be sparkly and bright together. Your quest for an external other feels like it's coming to completion, and because of your early patterning everything about the situation screams "YES!"

There might be some early glimpses of the toxic mess that's about to come your way – but sometimes there aren't. Sometimes, we go bravely into love believing all future promises and believing our own bullshit – that we need a savior. It's okay – really – just brace yourself.

As the shiny newness begins to fade the toxicity starts to show up. The nastiness gets nastier, and you find yourself on guard. Because of how good the good parts were, you now begin to reinvest in your bad investment.

You drank the poison with a smile on your face, willingly – like wine, as you handed your power over.

Writing Prompts & Things to Ponder

Have you secretly wanted a rescue at a time when you chose at toxic partner?

Do you recall a specific argument where things definitely changed from 'just a spat' to potentially dangerous?

Are there people in your life who definitely feel safe? Describe the relationship and how you feel in it.

Chapter 2

Friends, Finances & Freedom

Chapter 2: Friends, Finances & Freedom

I hope your head didn't jerk this soon into the book, because here we are. As a divorcee of 22 years, having married one of the most toxic people I've ever met, this first chapter sums up my five years being married.

First, it was the isolation from my family, his disdain for my family no matter how nice they were, and his overbearing control of my time, which left me no autonomy to have my own friends.

They might be toxic if they're controlling your freedom. I still recall my excitement as I discovered my talents and grew in my career. Every time I came home with good news of a promotion or raise his little toxic comments would flare up, "Do you really think women are supposed to make more than men? Are you just doing this so you can leave me?"

These items are not intended to be a way for you to lie, hide information, or be manipulative within your relationship – and while transparency is a goal when we are in safe relationships, in a toxic relationship actions that *should* be safe often are not, and that is the purpose of this discussion.

They might be toxic if they are attempting to control:

- Your basic freedom.
- How you look or dress.
- Who you associate with in your free time.
- Your ability to save or earn money.
- Your income or finances or how you spend.
- Where you go.
- Your private email, phone, computer, vehicle or other transportation.
- What you eat, when you exercise, or how your body looks.

In my marriage, my ambitions were never just ambitions. They were perceived as personal attacks or competition. At this age, I was young and we only had one bank account – so it all went to the same place. Even though I paid on his debt our entire marriage me making more money was ridiculous to him. "This," as far as he was concerned, was as far as I was going to get.

Getting my degree was absolutely out of the question and was in no way a good investment. I mean, can you imagine educating a Hispanic woman? My equally toxic mother-in-law, Brenda, often reminded me that I was "just a Mexican" – whatever the fuck that meant – I understood, at the very least, how he inherited his ignorance – making it no more acceptable.

I can't imagine trying to have a side hustle next to him, or ever starting a business where he was not the center of attention.

He was never my 'Ride or Die' and he was definitely not in my corner, unless he was backing me into it.

No one behavior will tell the whole story – and some people doing some of these things some of the time does not automatically mean anything. This book is a tool to sharpen your discernment – and for many it may be your first exposure to the eye-opening experience of discovering these patterns in your life.

When you decide to heal, the universe will have your back.

Writing Prompts & Things to Ponder

What type of reactions do you get when you discuss future plans and dreams with someone toxic?

Do you feel like you're stifled in your personal growth due to an outside person's comments or behavior?

Are there people in your life who you can share your dreams with? Describe the relationship and how you feel in it.

Chapter 3

Trust, And the Lack Thereof

Chapter 3: Trust, And the Lack Thereof.

Speaking of my toxic ex-mother-in-law I still remember early in the marriage when I was still willing to be around her. This was early in my years of discovering toxic relationships and boundaries.

My ex-husband, despite being one of the co-stars of this book was actually a very intelligent guy, and he was really good at his job – a mechanic, at the time. We'd met while he was in college. One afternoon at lunch Brenda commented, "he could've never gotten straight As – she (me) must've hacked into their computer system and changed your grades." She peered down her pointy nose at me with her ridiculous looking Martha-Stewart-looking outfit.

In the early 2000s we didn't have Karens we had Brendas. I feel like Saturday Night Live probably did an impression of her type.

They might be toxic if you are not trusted:

- When you're just being yourself.
- When you've accomplished something.
- To manage your own life within the context of the partnership.
- To have your own schedule, vehicle, plans, friends, etc.
- To fix things in your own life like a job loss or change, a budget, a financial decision.
- To go places alone, to have your own social media accounts, or other basic privacies.
- To make future plans for your own self-improvement. (see next chapter)

Writing Prompts & Things to Ponder

Has a toxic person in your life made up an inaccurate or exaggerated narrative about you that they refuse to let go of? What kinds of remarks do they make?

Are you accused of things you couldn't even dream up yourself? Describe them.

What are some of the insults that replay in your head? Can you identify who they came from or when they were said to you? Can you affirm that they are not true by looking at the quality of your life?

THEY MIGHT BE TOXIC

Chapter 4

Sabotage vs. Success

Chapter 4: Sabotage vs. Success

For most of us, we self-sabotage until we don't – it's part of growing up for many. Once we decide to stop our own self-sabotaging behaviors, we may find that external forces are now there for us to notice. I am not suggesting that every time someone offers you a cheat meal while you're dieting that it's intentional sabotage, or that you need to run from the relationship – the key is discernment of pattern – do they do it all the time? Are there snide little remarks?

When it comes to success or sabotage, they might be toxic if:

- Your wins are seen as a threat.
- You are discouraged from healthy self-improvement with "I like you just how you are."
- Your job or profession is referred to as "just a ____."
- You are spoken to in hyperbole – "You'll always be ____." Or "You'll never be ____."
- They're afraid of your growth.
- You can't be honest with them about future goals or plans.

Some very real examples of things that have been said to me and others, etc. in this style might include things like:

- "I always thought you were gorgeous with longer hair, that's why I told you I loved it really short – I didn't want other men looking at you."
- "I didn't marry you for _____."
- "You're just a glorified _____."
- "You're just losing weight so you can leave me."
- "Why would you waste money on a degree?"

We don't need anyone in our lives to create more negative self-talk. If someone is making you question your own efforts, your own abilities, your gifts or talents – run, don't walk.

We all change and grow, and it's quite natural, but in these types of relationships someone gaining self-esteem is a threat to the dysfunction that everyone is comfortable with.

Writing Prompts & Things to Ponder

Identify the bullshit insults that have been thrown at you for what they are. Write them down, and affirm that they do not belong to you, but to the person who believes this about themselves.

Chapter 5

Make Up My Mind: Unsolicited Advice,

Life Management, Etc.

Chapter 5: Make Up My Mind: Unsolicited Advice, Life Management, etc.

I am not a therapist, so if there's another official name for this control style, I am unaware of it – though some of it may fall under the term gaslighting. This section comes from my personal relationship mistakes and subsequent learning as well as observing others in similar situations.

In short, being controlled by another person – unless we have consciously chosen to hand over some administrative role of a relationship is control. Kids or those still living at home with parents: this does not apply to your parents making rules for your safety and wellbeing, etc., or in cases where two people are sharing a bank account and BOTH are required to be responsible and transparent.

Being controlled is absolutely toxic, and it might look like:

- Any of the items listed in previous chapters.
- Comments made under the breath, in sarcasm, or stabbing remarks followed by "I was just joking."
- Having no privacy.
- Avoiding sharing news to avoid the "Do you know what I think you should do?"
- Having your journal read, bank account or phone monitored constantly, emails and passwords shared.
- Not being allowed to ask questions, or being given answers that are half-assed, secretive, or otherwise invasive or manipulative.
- One person in the relationship being afforded privacy while others are not.
- Being forced to share a vehicle when finances permit a second one.
- Having tracking devices or software unknowingly installed. *I will reiterate here – if you are underage and live with parents, they have every right to monitor your activity in order to keep you safe. If you are an employee using company equipment, the same applies.* This item is intended for adults in adult relationships where personal privacy is an expectation.

Writing Prompts & Things to Ponder

Describe a time that you shared great news or a big idea with someone, and because of their comments you decided not to go after your dream or goal. What could you have said to them instead?

THEY MIGHT BE TOXIC

Chapter 6

Gifts With Expectations & Future Faking

Chapter 6: Gifts With Expectations and Future Faking.

This chapter needs little to no explanation – however using gifts as manipulation is all too common. Either there is a future promise of a gift, and that future promise is the means to control you in the present – or – a gift is given but the receipt of that gift comes with conditions that you had no say in.

For example: you're an introvert, and there is a certain amount of time that you are willing to spend with family – maybe it's once a month, a few times a month, or a few times a year. The amount does not matter. A gift is given, and as it is given, during your enamor, the expectations are also shared:

- "I'm giving you this gift, but I expect you to spend more time with the family."

There's intrinsically nothing wrong with family wanting more time in most cases – but in this case, as a core part of the personality of having energetic limits on how time will be spent, it's being asked that the person change the core of who they are.

Let's rephrase what they're saying to you:

- *"This gift comes with strings. I've decided to give you xyz, and because I think xyz is a big deal, you need to do what makes me comfortable, and ignore what makes you comfortable. I am making a sacrifice for you, and now I am expecting a sacrifice in return. This gift comes with strings.* When you decide to violate those strings I will perceive an offense or deficit. I gave you a gift. You did not submit to my wishes – therefore you don't give a crap about me, the relationship, the family, etc."

Because you did not change as a person due to this gift, now the gift becomes a grudge. It's brought up any chance you need to be reminded of your dues. It may be described as "how you acted when I did x for you."

Gifts are supposed to come with joy, not strings.

Writing Prompts & Things to Ponder

Describe a time when someone made promises of a future vacation, a future purchase, a future child or relationship, a future promotion, etc. as a way to manipulate you.

What would you do differently if this scenario arose again in the future?

THEY MIGHT BE TOXIC

Chapter 7

Domineering Communications

Chapter 7: Domineering Communications

I once heard someone say, it is not money that is the root of all evil, it's the lack of communication. It made me chuckle – but really, trying to debate the righteous is a fruitless effort. Even the word itself-righteous – *right*eous-ness, the refusal to have a two-way conversation that involves listening and learning.

When one is right, there's no room to learn. There's a very visual way to tell this story:

> "Never wrestle with a pig.
> You'll both get dirty, but the pig will enjoy it."

This is the epitome of trying to debate the righteous – you're knocked out of emotional balance and as you try to regain your footing the proverbial rug is yanked from underneath your feet.

You're left on your tail and they're still laughing about it. This is not safe communication. They might be toxic if:

- They bring up a serious issue at a time where the conversation can't be completed, like before walking into a family gathering.
- You've answered a series of questions where you feel you've unknowingly dug yourself into a hole, but all you did was answer honestly.
- There's no room to share your opinion, viewpoint, etc.
- You're expected to keep secrets about what goes on behind closed doors.
- You're treated one way in public, and another way in private – often exaggerated public displays of affection mixed with explosive arguments in private.
- You're walking on eggshells all the time.
- You're only allowed to call or text at specific times.
- You're asked to do something, and when you do it you're told all the reasons that was a dumb thing to do.

There are many common phrases and lines of conversation in this vein. They might be toxic if you hear things like:

- Can't you do anything right?
- Can you really be that dumb?
- Are you even trying?
- What kind of _____ would do something so stupid?
- References to wasting their precious time, money resources, etc.
- Insults about mental health status, sexual orientation, religious or personal beliefs.
- Belittling of the things that make you, you – how you dress or act, your personality, your likes and dislikes.

The language of the toxic is intended to make you feel small - insults that land in your head, and stick to your thighs for a decade, until you realize you've been repeating them to yourself, even though you left – even though you got out.

These patterns are not easy to break. You might find that they span through personal relationships of all kinds: romantic, friendships, work, and any other place you let them. This is your shadow work to do – and only you can discover how the patterns arose, and why you may still be drawn to this personality type.

Are you starting to see it? Are you seeing signs of some of these things in yourself, in the relationships of family members or close friends?

Once you begin to see it, you can't unsee it.

Writing Prompts & Things to Ponder

What are some toxic comments that replay in your mind? When do they come up? Can you identify who first said them to you?

Are you able to separate yourself from these phrases and realize that they do not belong to you?

Chapter 8

Blame Games / Word Games

Chapter 8: Blame Games / Word Games

Is everything your fault even when it's not? Of course, it is! Blame games go right along with word games – and may fall into the category of gaslighting.

Gaslighting, specifically is a behavior where you are told you're not perceiving what you're perceiving. You begin to feel crazy in your own views. The term comes from a classic film where an abusive husband is lowering the lighting in the house, at the time they were gas lamps. In the film, the wife claimed that the lights were getting dimmer and dimmer by the day, but the husband refused to agree, even though he was the one dimming the lights.

Essentially, we're asked to agree with an untrue version of reality: "I didn't insult you, you just got offended over nothing."

Apologies in the flavor of "Sorry you got mad," instead of "Sorry for how I acted," might sound familiar.

Our actions, reactions and behavior are ours and ours alone. How we act, how we react, and how we behave isn't because of someone else, but because of our own self – we must own that and be responsible for it. We've all been through difficulty, it's not an excuse to act like a jerk - quite the contrary, it's an invitation to be and do better.

Blame and word games might sound like:

- A series of events to create a blame story. "If you hadn't done this, then I wouldn't have done that."
- Look what you made me do
- You make me feel _____.
- More hyperbole. Words like – make, always, never, everything.
- Childish phrases: "You started it." "Because of how you looked at me."

One of the most powerful lessons I learned in this specific area was from Brené Brown, author of many amazing books, public speaker, and all around badass – in several of her books she uses a question for herself when she finds herself playing thoughts of blame in her mind. "The story that I'm telling myself is _____."

This powerful phrase empowers us to see our own story – and puts the responsibility of good communication on us, instead of charging into a fight with assumptions. Here's what a conversation like this might sound like.

"The story I'm telling myself is that, when you made a face at my comment and crossed your arms, I assumed your disdain was about me or how I acted."

"The story I'm telling myself when you're late is that you don't care about my time, and that your time is more valuable than mine."

The reality is, a person's body language or lateness could be for a variety of reasons – but instead we've chosen our own narrative and assumed it was true. People are people – we forget things, we live in physical bodies, many of us wear our emotions on our sleeves – and honestly not all of us are wonderfully skilled communicators.

I love Brené Brown's work because she will share active situations that are difficult – real stories that make us realize in moments of our shadow arising to greet us we get to choose – it's the classic "Choose your own story" book – and we get to write the end – and all the middle parts too!

When we decide to address not only our feelings and emotions, but also the underlying story, we soon realize that there are other ways to communicate. If you were in an abusive conversation and tried this with your partner what would happen? Do they have the emotional maturity to take a step like this with you?

Personally, I can't imagine any of my abusive ex people having the ability or desire to do that – whether a boss, sibling, or romantic partner.

If you've allowed the abuse during the entire duration of a marriage or relationship, disrupting the patterns can be difficult – but also dangerous, and sometimes impossible. Don't expect people to change because you've learned something new. **If you need to remove yourself from a situation, do that as safely as possible.**

THEY MIGHT BE TOXIC

Writing Prompts & Things to Ponder

If you've tried to set boundaries and it hasn't worked, what are some ways you could energetically separate yourself from the toxic people or situations in your life?

Could you care less, engage less, talk about it less, see them less? Could you share less or respond less? Can you safely make exit plans?

"You can't change the people around you. But you can change the people around you."

Joshua Fields Millburn

"Don't believe everything you think."

Robert Fulgrum

THEY MIGHT BE TOXIC

Chapter 9

Sharing & Safety

Chapter 9: Sharing & Safety

A healthy relationship is where we go to find support, comradery, safety, joy, and guidance. A healthy relationship is solace and safety in a wide, wide range of scenarios.

When I call my best friend to share good news she is always over the moon for me. She celebrates my wins, and I celebrate her wins. I grieve her losses, and we are able to ebb and flow in a way that rarely needs to be managed.

If you feel unsafe asking questions, sharing good news, future plans, new ideas, or even bad news, they might be toxic. They also might be toxic if they:

- Assume that you can't be successful at anything new.
- Put your ideas down.
- See themselves as the only capable person in the relationship.
- Are uninterested in celebrating good things that happen for you.
- Belittle your business or creative ideas.
- Only see the old version of you, and not the current version.
- Won't make time to support you when you receive bad news.
- Don't want to brainstorm ways to move forward when something goes sideways.
- Don't seem like they're in your corner unless they're backing you into it.
- Punish you or withhold (affection, finances, etc.) in response to setting boundaries or for speaking up.

Asking to feel safe in a relationship *is not too much to ask for*. Nobody is suggesting that life comes without discomforts. Life, indeed comes with many discomforts – let's get that out of the way, first and foremost. Discomforts are necessary for our growth.

Asking to feel safe simply means you have room to grow, make mistakes, dream, share and become whatever version of you comes next. It means being able to bring up the uncomfortable, the wonderful, the unknown, and the known.

Relationships change over time, and trust is built one insignificant moment after another, repetition being the key. As a person shows their consistent behavior over time, you learn how safe (or not) you are.

You might not feel safe if you are:

- Making yourself smaller in your accomplishments, goals, or desires for your own happiness and contentment.
- Afraid to be your authentic self.
- Accustomed to being belittled, made fun of or insulted no matter how directly or indirectly the words.
- Constantly feeling defensive.
- Feel like you can't ask questions.
- Censoring what you say to avoid reactions.
- Being told how or when to speak, what to say or not say, or find yourself controlling those things to avoid reactions.
- Unable to laugh, have fun, and be yourself.

Please also consider that some things, for example, being defensive – *can and do come from the self* – but if you feel defensive all the time with one person, regardless of the subject there may be something deeper to be looked at. None of these items alone tell the whole story.

Your own patterns will reveal themselves to you as you do this work. Forgive yourself, and use what you learn to create better, more empowering relationships. They don't always have to be romantic relationships – you can start by building up a current friendship.

Writing Prompts & Things to Ponder

Describe a time where you took someone's nasty comments and used them to talk yourself out of moving forward in your life.

Are you still in belief of someone else's limiting beliefs or insulting comments?

Chapter 10:

Mind Reading & People-Pleasing

Chapter 10: Mind Reading & People-Pleasing

Get out your crystal ball – because ***damn you should've known that!***

- Are you expected to know the future, anticipate their needs, coddle every whim and desire?
- Do their needs come before everyone else's?
- Walk on eggshells much?
- Do their insults replay in your head?
- Do they take up a significant amount of space in your thoughts?
- Did you ***know damn well*** that you shouldn't have done that?
- Did you even think about what you said before you said it?

All sarcasm aside, people pleasing is one of the core markers of co-dependency. Essentially your happiness is tied to the happiness of others. This is behavior that is beyond normal caretaking or caregiving.

You may subconsciously believe that if you can avoid lighting your angry partner's very short fuse that you will get to live in peace. The reality is, your toxic partner does not want peace and until you really do, you will continue to do the dance, and drink the poison. The empath narcissist bond is as old as time.

Just like every buyer needs a seller, every abuser needs a willing partner. This may feel like a slap in the face. It was intended to. Just so you know – I have been that willing partner more times than I care to admit. Less often in romantic situations, and more often in business and family – but it's happened in every single area of my life.

I am not immune. I am merely sending a smoke signal.

Writing Prompts & Things to Ponder

Setting boundaries is a great tool. It may require repeating the information more than once as the person learns your boundaries.

Do you know how to create healthy boundaries when you are in new relationships with friends, coworkers, and romantic partners?

How might a toxic person react to boundary setting?

THEY MIGHT BE TOXIC

Chapter 11

Deal With It

Chapter 11: Deal with it.

Are you expected to give a free pass to overtly abusive behavior?

You see it when he kicks the dog or screams at your two-year old. You see it when he uses a derogatory word about someone who is similar to you in some way. You see it when he controls you with a look.

Abuse is not just one thing. It may be physical; it may not be. It could be verbal, mental, or physical or any combination thereof, on any given day. It might come with a side of laughter and a comment about how sensitive you are. It might come with a backhand and a bruise. Just because one of these actions leaves a mark and has laws to protect you does NOT mean that the other forms are not relevant.

Please let that not be understated. In the 2022 Netflix Series 'The Maid' her toxic husband smashes a glass vase next to hear head on the wall. If you believe that it's not abuse because he never hit her, I hope that you've been robbed of your cognitive dissonance, and that your eyes are fully open, no matter how headfucked you feel right now.

Don't forget – the toxic can be:

- Beautiful, charming, or successful people.
- Friends
- Bosses
- A culture (or a cult)
- Your sibling
- Parents, and grandparents
- Religious leaders
- Politicians
- Seemingly innocent, and only situationally abusive.
- Outwardly charming, even kind-seeming.
- Detrimental to your wellbeing.

Writing Prompts & Things to Ponder

Are you beginning to notice patterns in your own toxic relationships?

Are there common traits that make you attracted to the person in the beginning?

Do you find yourself having exaggerated reactions around a specific person? What do you think this might mean?

Closing Thoughts

There are no all-inclusive lists of the crazymaking behaviors of narcissism, codependency, and unhealed trauma. Surely, I've missed at least a hundred.

Your body knows it. Your nervous system knows it. Every cell of your being eventually screams it.

As someone who got to the other side of it – there is another side. There are also endless practice sessions and refresher courses available as well – they could be anywhere. One could show up tomorrow.

My advice to you on this day is this: Remember that you haven't left a situation until you've left the situation. Recognizing it isn't the same as making a change. You may not have all the answers today for how that change will come to fruition – just know that if you are open to solutions the universe will enjoy surprising you with them.

Be well.

Shine bright.

It was never your fault.

ABOUT THE AUTHOR

Maria Colomy is the Author of They Might Be Toxic, and one of the co-founders of the "They Might Be Toxic" podcast and brand. Maria has had a vast, colorful career that always involved writing. She has also had a colorful life, that often involves toxic relationships and the continuing realization that much like art, or writing, managing our relationships is also a skill that we need to constantly improve.

THEY MIGHT BE TOXIC

THEY MIGHT BE TOXIC

www.ingramcontent.com/pod-product-compliance
Lightning Source LLC
Chambersburg PA
CBHW022105020426
42335CB00012B/845

9 798987 279090